Here and Now

A Whimsical Take On God

Illustrations and text by

Jeff Stilwell

© Jeff Stilwell Studio 2014

ISBN: 978-0-578-40771-5

Library of Congress Registration Number Txu 1-921-792

JeffStilwell.com

(My friend Thrashin' Jack is coming along for the ride.)

(So is Lotus.)

- 1 -
The Idea That Worked

In the beginning it was simple. We needed a God. So we created one.

In fact, we created many. All across Mesopotamia - that place on the globe where the Tigris and Euphrates meet - in a land long ago called Ur, creating Gods was all the rage.

And why not? Gods are useful. You can explain things with Gods, such as why lightning hits a tree (God is angry), or why it's raining (God is sad), or why it's thundering (God is at the roller derby) or why there's a rainbow (God is feeling artistically bohemian) or why somebody dies (God wants them back). Gods are useful.

In Ur, where creating Gods became the new fad, every town had one. To show off their particular God, each town set up a temple. Each took great pains to make sure their hometown temple was different from all the others'. It was important. For example, they designed their own symbols representing their hometown God and carved it into billboards (made of stone, we call them steles).

Three circles around, then offer the bird.

They also designed their own, distinctive, hometown rituals to worship their hometown Gods in their hometown temples. And if all the rituals across Ur looked more or less the same to a foreigner, a local could pick out the details – one here, one there – that made one town's ritual crucially different from another's. It was important.

To staff these temples and ensure these crucial details in the ritual were performed properly, each town selected and trained a group of (mostly) men. These (mostly) men became known as priests. The towns also passed laws saying that none but the priests could perform the rituals correctly. It was important.

After all, there was (and is) a lot of money in being known for having the magic formula that makes God answer your prayers. For example, the ritual at the temple in Nippur might say that to ask its God for a promotion at work, you needed to purchase two doves, without blemish, at the marketplace so the priests could slaughter and burn them on a special altar at the temple.

If the ritual didn't work the first time around, you could usually go buy a second pair of doves and do it again. Or you could even up the ante a bit and buy a pair of larger, more impressive-looking animals, so long as they, too, were without blemish.

(pssst!)

A skatepark for the temple? Umm...

Sometimes, however, no matter how large and impressive a pair of animals you purchased and had slaughtered and burned, God didn't answer your prayers. At this point, the priests helpfully explained that you were on the bad side of God and that you would need to do something special to get back on God's good side. Such special projects were often difficult, even really quite expensive, such as funding a new porch for the temple or setting up a pension plan for the priesthood's retirement someday.

Nevertheless, usually everything came to rights, eventually. It worked. This idea – the God idea – worked so well in Ur that neighboring classical Greece decided they needed their own hometown Gods, too. Way off in India and China, municipal leaders came to the same conclusion. Pretty soon everybody who was anybody could boast a hometown God. It was important.

It was also useful. Because while times on the whole in Ur were pretty peaceful, occasionally the local rowdies of a given town would get, well, rowdy. At that point, they would get liquored up on a Friday night, "borrow" the chariot from their parents and do a smash-and-grab on the neighboring towns. The rowdies would steal some of the neighboring town's wheat, some of their livestock and, though it's hard to say, some of their virgins.

Knowing this, the leaders of every town went to incredible lengths to brag about the prowess of their local God. After all, even liquored up young rowdies go for easy pickings.

In fact, just as professional athletes today compete regularly – up this week, down the next – for the top rank in their given sport so the hometown Gods in Ur competed for the top rank of the biggest, baddest God of them all. At least the towns said so. And it was quite a discussion.

Eventually a new voice was added to the mix, at least for a while: A man named Zoroaster in a neighboring land said that he thought all these made up Gods were silly. He believed that there really was just One True God, above all the others, invented or otherwise. At this, the towns in Ur laughed themselves silly and discarded Zoroaster as a nutcase.

Interestingly, however, Zoroaster packaged his One True God with a very attractive accessory: Heaven. Zoroaster claimed that when we died, if we were on the right side of his One True God, then we could "live" forever in his One True God's Heaven.

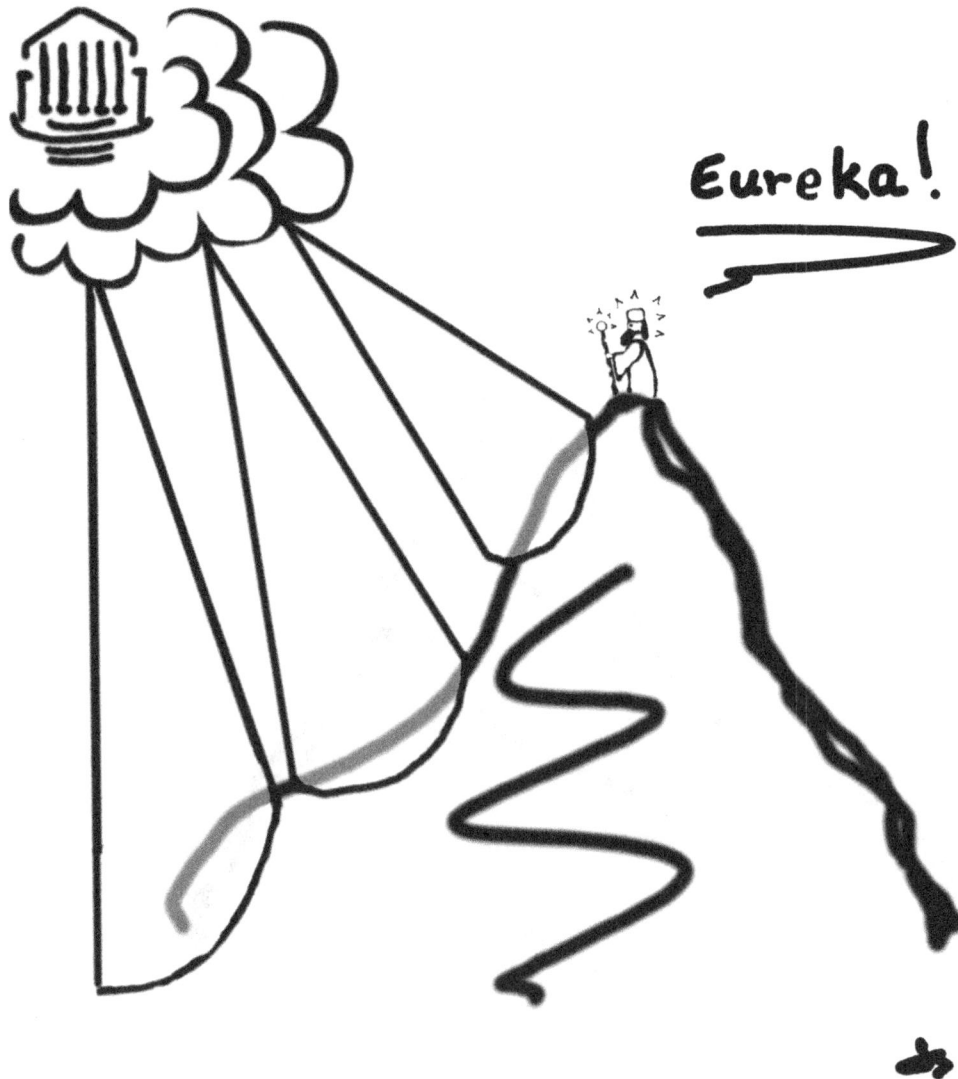

This was a revolutionary concept. And an attractive one.

After all, who doesn't want to "live" forever? Up to that point, everyone assumed that when we died, just like last fall's harvest plowed under, we became hungry ghosts living in the ground. Not great, but we did have our time, didn't we?

Zoroaster's Heaven was a game-changer. If the towns in Ur still laughed him off, they weren't laughing so loudly anymore. And they stopped laughing completely when a group of rowdies began their smash-and-grabs at a pitch unknown before.

These rowdies, called Persians, were just poor hill-country folk. But they certainly knew their smash-and-grab techniques. Besides, they even had Zoroaster's One True God with the promise of Heaven on their side. They fought more fiercely, taking greater risks than the people in the towns all across Ur. And why not? If the Persians died, they knew they were going to their One True God's Heaven.

What kind of Heaven did the hometown Gods of Ur have to offer? None.

Eventually, the Persians swept over all of Mesopotamia, doing smash-and-grabs every Friday night. More importantly, they decided to stay. This, too, was revolutionary. Everyone knew that after a good smash-and-grab, you were supposed to take your stolen wheat, livestock and virgins home with you. The Persians stayed.

And their new-fangled One True God with his Heaven became all the rage. In fact, it became so popular that neighboring classical Greece and all the way over in India and China, the One True God idea took root, too. (Under different names, of course.)

This idea has come down to us this day.

- 2 -
The Idea That Worked (A Little Longer)

Things got a lot more complicated after that. Almost artistically more complex. First, the Persians took their chariots all the way to the sea, conquering every people they found in their path. Every people they conquered got tied up and shipped back to Ur to live. And every people they conquered learned about, in one way or another, Zoraster's One True God and his Heaven.

After two generations of living in Ur, one group of these conquered peoples decided to return to the land from which they had been taken. This land, called Israel, lay right on the coast of the Med(iterranean Sea). These people were called Hebrews. They liked the One True God with his Heaven idea so much that when they traveled back to Israel, they brought the idea with them.

And there this new idea flourished. There was some backwriting into the official books, of course, to make the One True God idea sound like it had always been a Hebrew notion from the very beginning. Nevertheless, it worked.

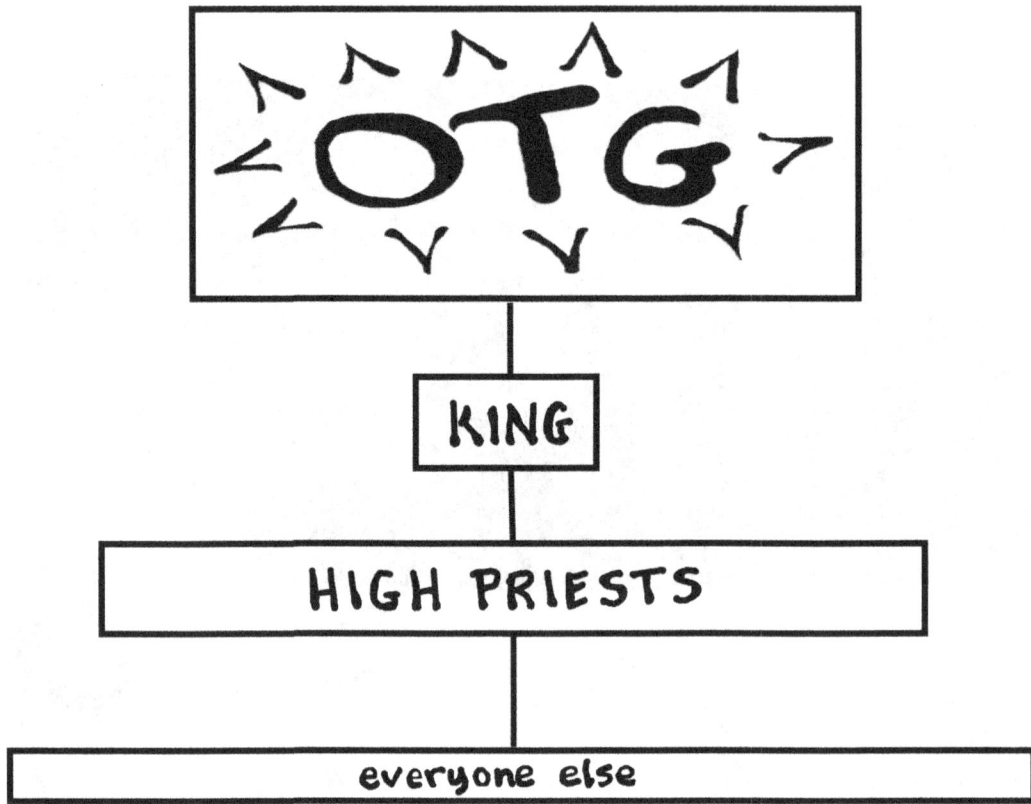

The One True God idea blossomed into a way of organizing the Hebrews around a king, a set of high priests and (below them) everyone else.

What's more, this new idea gave rise to a whole different viewpoint, for another new voice was added to the mix, at least for a while. This young man, Jesus, saw himself as having a special relationship with this One True God, so special that not even the high priests in the capital city could claim a better one.

Needless to say, the high priests were a little bit upset at this challenge to their exalted position in the community. So, they arranged to get rid of him.
They were successful.

Left alone, Jesus' followers became very sad. In their sadness, moreover, they decided that Jesus was right – that he was special. So special that, rather than simply dying when he was gotten rid of, instead, something wonderful must have happened to him.

In fact, they decided that, rather than disappearing forever like normal people do, Jesus must still be around somewhere, maybe even living alongside the One True God in Heaven as some sort of Assistant One True God.

They couldn't see Jesus, of course. They had to believe he was there.

Then, too, this was a bit confusing because you can't very well have two One True Gods sitting side by side for very long. After all, to which One True God do you pray to make it rain, for example? Especially if, as the Hebrews decided, their One True God was a jealous one.

So, among the Jesus followers over the centuries, there have been many arguments about this whole One True God/Two True Gods/One True God with an Assistant One True God question. Indeed, those arguments continue down to the present day.

Nevertheless, the Jesus idea worked.

Meanwhile, another new voice was added to the mix, at least for a while. This young man, Mohammed, saw himself as having a special relationship with the One True God, so special that not even the local priests in his neighborhood could claim a better one.

Needless to say, the local priests in his neighborhood were a little bit upset at this challenge to their exalted position in the community. So, they arranged to get rid of him. They were unsuccessful.

Unlike Jesus, Mohammed got tipped off in advance. He and his followers ran. They ran so far, they moved to an entirely different city, where they knew no one. In fact, Mohammed's very first friends when he got there were some Hebrews living on the next block. (Which makes you think.)

Mohammed thought the whole One True God/Two True Gods/One True God with an Assistant One True God question silly. As far as he was concerned, Jesus was just like he was, a gifted young man with a special relationship to the One True God. And that was enough.

IT NEEDS SOMETHING...

Then, too, because Mohammed, unlike Jesus, managed to live long enough to see his ideas put into action, he created a whole new community that could live out this special relationship with the One True God. Of course, just as the towns in ancient Ur did, with their desire to make their temples stand out, Mohammed decided to make his community special, different from everyone else.

For example, the Hebrews always got together in their buildings – called synagogues –
on Saturdays. The Jesus followers always got together in their buildings – called
churches – on Sundays. So, Mohammed decided to have his followers get together in a
new kind of building that he designed – called a mosque – on the only day left in the
weekend, Fridays.

Then, too, when it came to talking with the One True God, the Hebrews always swayed on their feet while praying. The Jesus followers always knelt, clasping their hands. So, Mohammed had his followers do something entirely different. He had his followers bow down, touching their foreheads to the earth, explaining that this was a good reminder to surrender to the One True God's will in their life.

It worked. The Mohammed idea worked quite well.

Indeed, over time, all three viewpoints – the Hebrews, the Jesus followers, and the Mohammed followers – became so distinctly different that they hardly understood one another. Yet, underneath all that difference lay the same idea, that of the One True God and his Heaven.

Interestingly, just as the rowdy Persians had, the Hebrews, the followers of Jesus, and the followers of Mohammed all figured out that the idea of a Heaven to go to after you die made it much easier to make war on others. They all realized this, much to their delight.

Thus, over the centuries, these three viewpoints have often gone to war on each other. Many, many, many have voluntarily died – not worried at all that they were cutting the only lives they would ever know drastically short – because they believed they were going to Heaven.

In fact, this idea works so well that all three viewpoints are making war on each other, even today.

- 3 -
Is The Idea Still Working?

Is it still working? Well, yes and no.

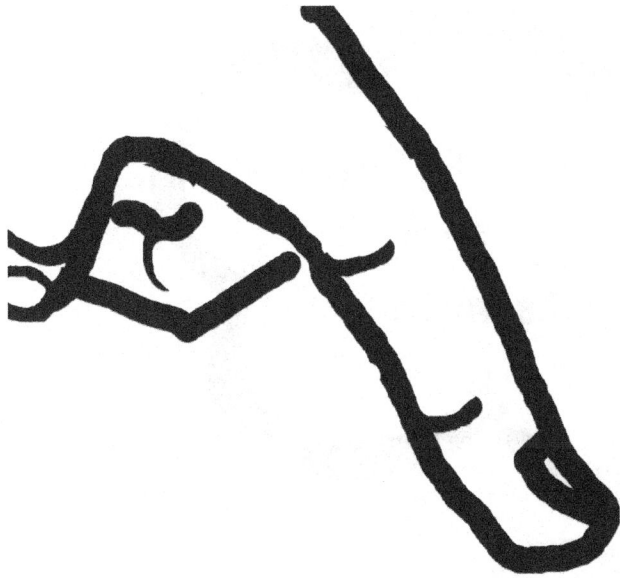

Yes, because Gods are always useful to explain things that we can't otherwise. Everything from why we get that raise at work (God was watching out for us and not the other guy) to why we got better from an illness (God made us healthy again) to why there is anything at all and not nothing (who else would create a Universe?).

On the other hand, the One True God idea is not working as well as it used to, if only because we understand so much more about the world around us. We know how things happen so regularly in nature that we don't have to create a God to explain them.

For example, we used to tell ourselves that God makes the rain happen. These days, we tend to think more in terms of warm fronts meeting cold fronts and the resulting precipitation getting pulled, through gravity, down to the surface of the earth.

In fact, it happens so regularly that we routinely predict when it will.

Much like we do with taking medicine to get better from an illness. We no longer need a God to take care of that problem anymore. Unless the illness is the kind for which we don't have any medicine yet. In that case, yes, we still turn to our One True God for help.

Is that fair? Not really. But when we're sick, or when someone we love is sick, we tend to turn a blind eye to little inconsistencies. It's human.

Nevertheless, as our understanding about the world around us continues to grow, our standards for what we find acceptable are changing. For example, it used to be that when a ship sank off the coast of some island halfway around the world, drowning many people in an awful tragedy, we didn't think too much about it. After all, it's not as if we knew them.

These days, however, we do think about it. In fact, we can't help but wonder why One True God didn't save them.

Three circles around, then offer the bird.

We might ask but, just as with the hometown Gods of Ur, we are not going to get an answer directly. For that, we have to go through a priest.

And here we run into yet one more problem. As our understanding about the world around us continues to grow, we find that there is not just one priest to turn to, as someone in Ur long ago would be limited to. No, we have all too many priests we can ask.

And they often disagree.

One priest might say that the people who drowned didn't pray the right prayer to One True God and, therefore, didn't deserve to be saved.

Another priest might say that those people are evil and, therefore, deserved to die in such a horrible manner.

A third priest might say that it's a mystery why One True God did not save those poor people. This doesn't really answer the question, but it might make us feel better.

A fourth priest might say that One True God is weeping with us about all those people who drowned. Which doesn't answer the question either, but it also might make us feel better.

For a while.

Still, our ability to comparison shop between the different answers offered by various priests does make us think a little more deeply on the whole question. It can't help but do so. After all, all four choices cannot be right. One must be right and the other three wrong.
Right?

Which do we choose and why? What a dilemma!

Well, most of us will choose the one that feels right for us (and immediately forget that there were other choices available). That doesn't make our choice right, of course. It just makes us feel like it is. It's human.

NUTHIN' DOING! = THUMB'S UP! = UMMM... = SOB!

A number of us will try to hold open the possibility that all the choices work, even if they clearly contradict one another. At least for a while. However, the longer we attempt this the harder it grows, so the dilemma usually gets dropped as quickly as possible (and then carefully forgotten).

A large number of us will try to escape the dilemma of having to make a choice altogether, thinking that One True God is above all earthly understanding. This works only so long as we choose to forget about the people who died tragically from a sinking ship because One True God would not save them.

After all, if One True God was not there for them when they needed help the most, why should One True God be there for us when we need help the most?

Put more gently, if One True God is beyond all understanding, how is that a comfort to anyone?

NUTHIN' DOING! <> THUMB'S UP! <> UMMM... <> SOB!

Last, a very, very few of us will admit the obvious: Since each possibility clearly contradicts the others...

Why couldn't all of them be wrong?

As if the priests, knowingly or not, are creating their own explanations for why One True God didn't save all those poor people from drowning. (In fact, any honest priest will admit he doesn't know why, but that he believes why.)

GOD	WAR	AGRIC.	FERTILITY	MINING
ANU	8	10	1	3
ENKI	2	9	4	1
ENLIL	7	3	?!	2
NABU	4	5		8
NINLIL	1	P		6
UTU	5			7

As soon as we draw this conclusion, we begin to think of all those Gods with all their accessories that have been created throughout all time, since the hometown Gods of Ur down to this day.

And, then we ask ourselves the inevitable question: Does this mean that we created the One True God we believe in, too? Just as so many others have in the past?

That means that the One True God we believe in is nothing more than a fantasy.

This also means that all the other accessories with which we packaged our One True God – such as the power to forgive, or justify, or purify, or judge, or punish, or reward, or create a Heaven for us to go to after we die – all these accessories are nothing more than fantasies, too.

This is another way in which the God Idea is not working very well anymore. Our old creations – our old Gods – just don't measure up to our current expectations.

All this said, however, there is still one way in which the God Idea does work. In fact, it works really well. Remember how Gods are useful for explaining things that we can't otherwise? The largest question of all – large enough to contain our entire universe – is why anything at all? Why is there anything? Why not nothing?

Our astrophysics, particularly our quantum physics, and our math tell us that the universe began with a Big Bang. (Of course, we always have to remind ourselves that the Big Bang is a mathematical model written out on a chalkboard somewhere; that we don't have anything like a webcam video showing the Big Bang making the universe so many billion years ago.)

So, when it comes to the largest question of all, our astrophysics, particularly our quantum physics, and our math can tell us how the universe began.

However, what they cannot do is tell us *why*.

That's where a God comes in handy. Gods are useful for explaining things that we can't otherwise.

Now, perhaps someday we will understand precisely why universes begin so well that we won't need a God to explain why ours began. In fact, we might even understand why universes begin so well – just as these days we understand the rain so well – that we might even start predicting the next time the universe will begin.

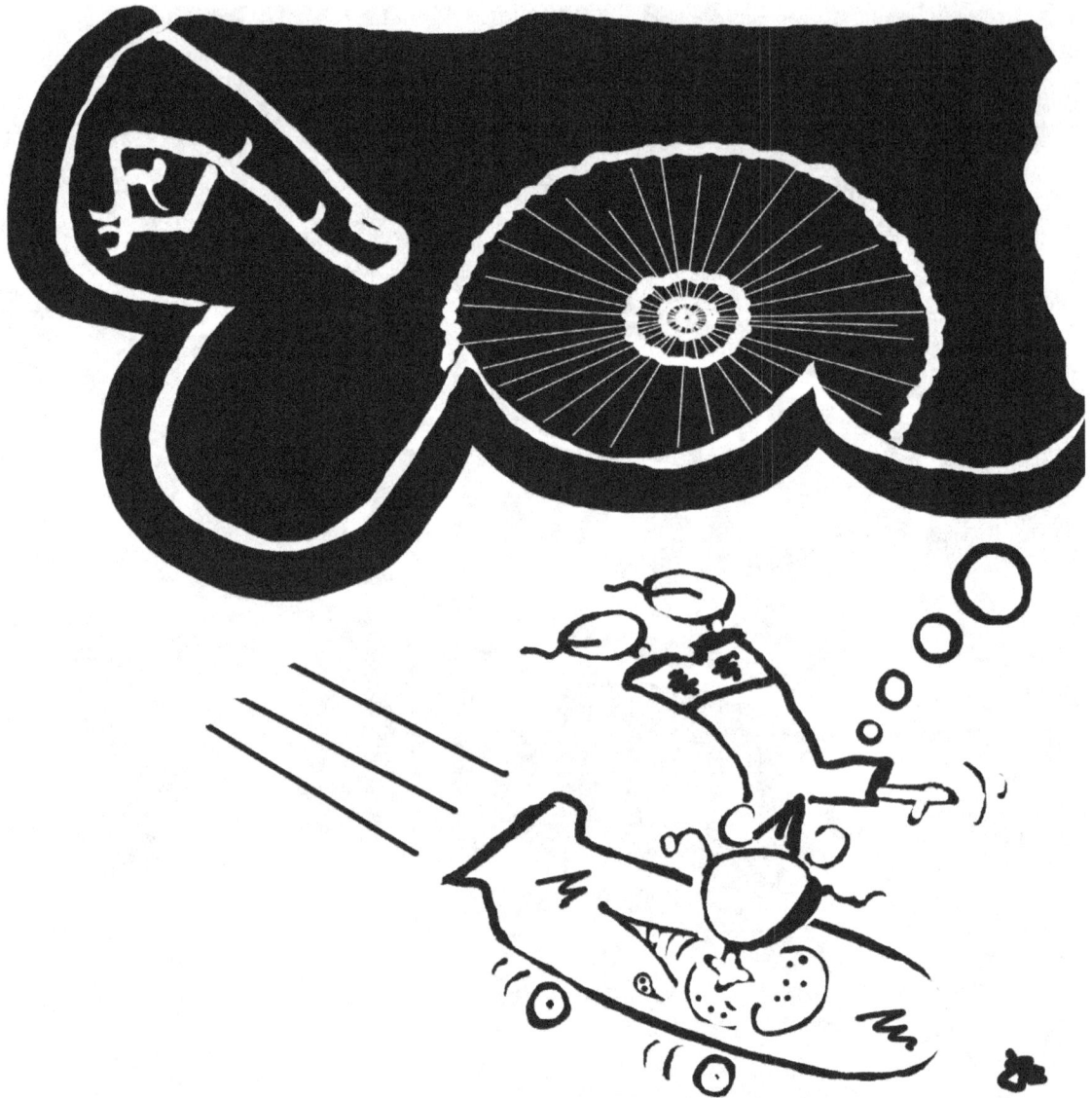

Until then, however, we shall have to make do with a God that we create to explain the beginning.

- 4 -
Here And Now

But, then, who wants to believe in a God that we ourselves create?

More to the point, how do we live our lives once we realize that the God we created is our own fantasy?

For example, what happens to our moral compass? Does it get skewed?

Then, too, if Heaven is just a fantasy we created, what happens after we die?

Interestingly enough, the longer we think about these two questions, the more we see they are related.

Let's do the moral compass, first. We freak out at the idea that our God-given ideas of good and evil are only fantasies. Yet, we should reassure ourselves that if they are only fantasies, they are our fantasies. That means, as we created Gods throughout all time to solve our problems for us, we created them in such a way that made the most sense to us.

Therefore, there is no reason to freak out. Our ideas of good and evil, our understandings of right and wrong are the same as they ever were. And why not? We created them.

The Heaven problem is a bit harder to swallow. If Heaven is just a fantasy that we created, what happens after we die? Well, the simple answer is...nothing.

We simply cease to exist. Our bodies get recycled along with last fall's harvest. Our thoughts, our memories – what we sometimes call our soul – all fade to nothing (unless we have recorded a few of them somewhere).

And that sounds perfectly awful. Doesn't it?

Until we remember that we are members of this universe. And, just like us, every member of this universe has a limited time. Planets, comets, asteroids, stars, solar systems, even whole galaxies all have a limited time. After that time, they all fade to nothing.

Put another way, everything that has come before us had a limited time, then faded to nothing, in part so that we could enjoy our limited time.

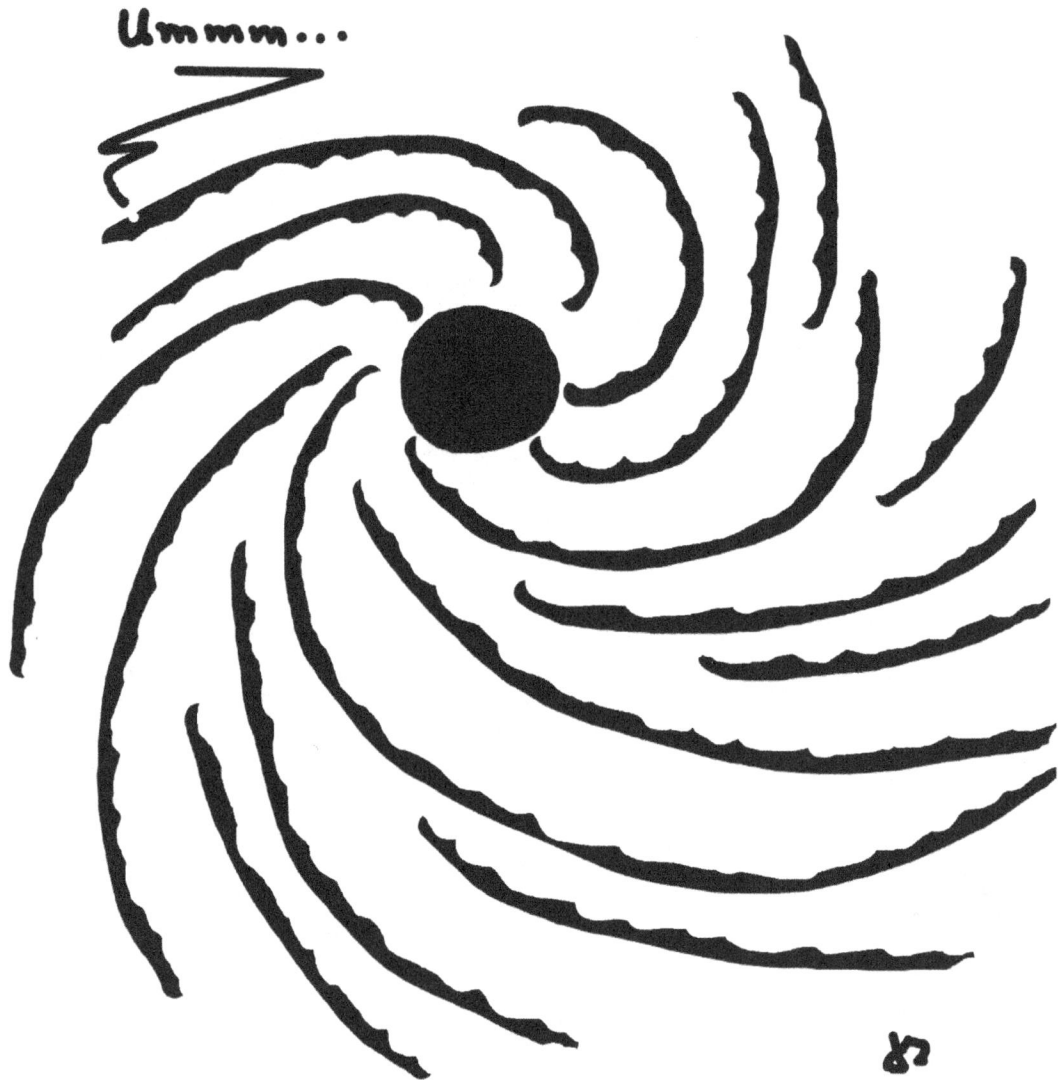

Why, at the very center of our own neighborhood, the Milky Way Galaxy, there is a dark star (some people prefer the name "black hole") recycling the nearby solar systems – solar systems just like ours – into new stars.

Why should we be any different?

At this point, our realization that Heaven is only a fantasy – that, instead, we have a limited time and then fade to nothing – stops sounding perfectly awful.

This is also the point where we realize that the two questions – of our moral compass and about Heaven – are closely related.

For, our focus shifts, in several ways.

First, the focus of our lives shifts from the someday to right here, right now. Instead of thinking about that mythical someday that we get to go to Heaven after we die (so long as we followed the rules), now we suddenly start paying more attention to what's happening in front of us. At this moment in time. In this place.

Each moment in time, each place.

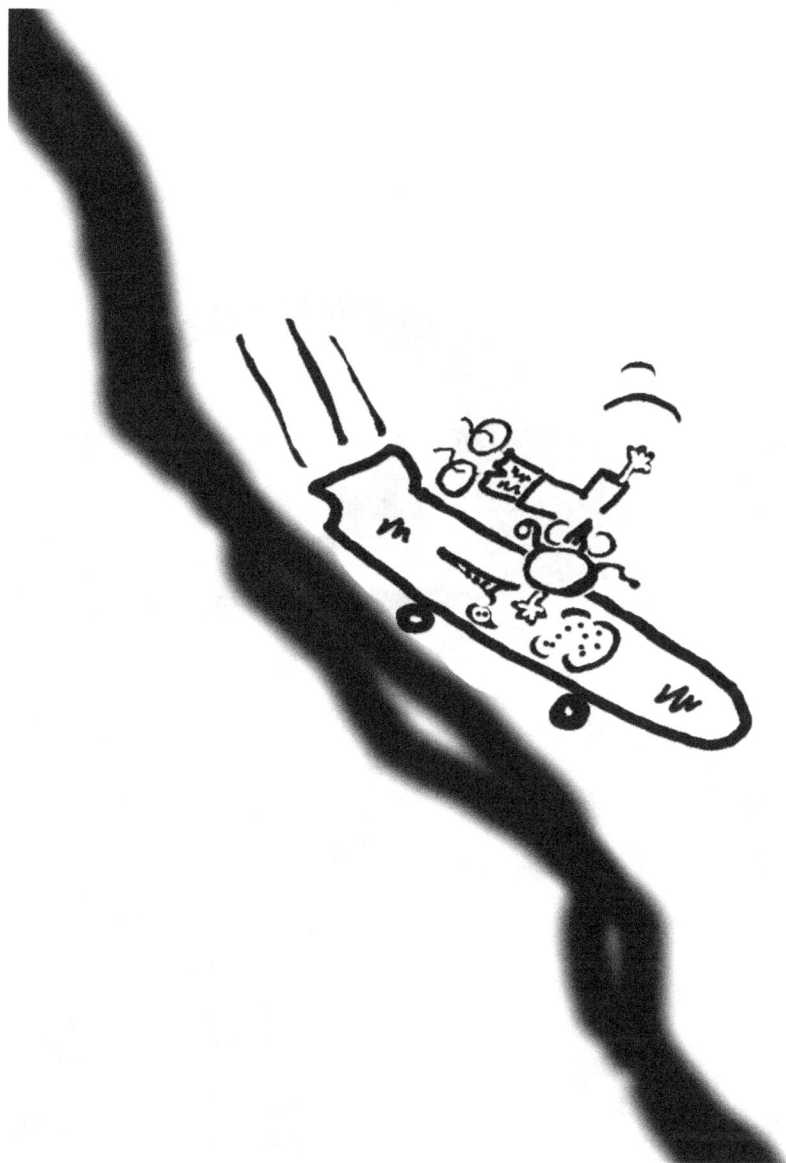

Here and now.

Then, too, the focus of our lives shifts quite naturally from making sure that we are following the Get Into Heaven rules to wondering how full our lives really are. As if, now that it dawns on us that we – like every other member of the universe – only get so much time, we had better make the most of it.

After all, whether a new born baby, a new born star, or a new born galaxy, the rule is the same: This is our time, use it well.

~

Exploring the fullest expression of meaning in my life.

~

Each of us can best decide how best to use our time well. And our answers will vary, widely. But, that's a really great thing about the universe: There is room enough for us all.

It is difficult though. It's hard to stay focused on each moment as it passes by.
Sometimes, we're so busy just enjoying the moment, we don't want to think about it. But
that's okay. It's not as if someone is going to punish us for not trying hard enough to
experience the fullness of our lives.

And that is the third way our focus shifts. Now that we realize that One True God is a fantasy, we become the prime motivator of our lives. We become motivated from within to explore as much of our lives as possible before it's time to fade away into nothing.

We become motivated to explore so much of our lives that when it is time to fade away, we look on the coming change with a sense of peace.

We don't feel cheated. We don't feel scared. We are simply, honestly grateful for the time we had.

We know that we used it well.

Okay, what do I do with all this?

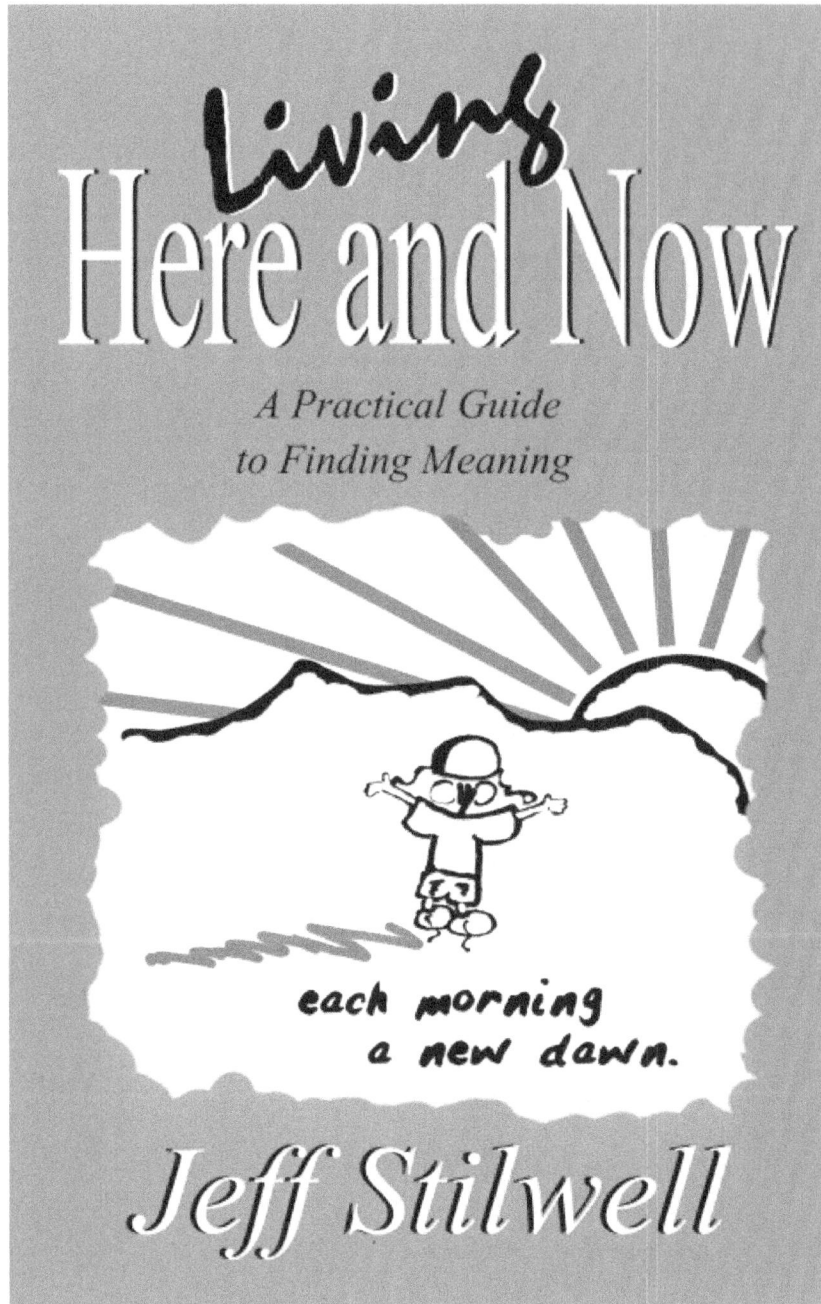

Living
Here and Now

*A Practical Guide
to Finding Meaning*

each morning
a new dawn.

Jeff Stilwell

Available on Amazon now.

Author Biography

Jeff Stilwell excels at the unexpected. Not content with his Midwestern roots, he found ways on the cheap to explore the wider world including selling gummy bears in high school to visit the Alps of central Europe. To pay for college, he worked a slime line as a head chopper in the clammy tundra of Alaska.

His thirst for adventure next took him to Asia where he studied Asian philosophy and the martial arts while exploring exotic locales including the Himalayas and the lands of Lord Jim, even surviving a squall in the Gulf of Siam.

His years in Asia deeply influenced his lifelong search for meaning, culminating later in his magnum opus, *Here and Now: A Whimsical Take On God.* In this illustrated work, his adorable cartoon character Thrashin' Jack leads the reader on the skateboard journey of humanity's creation of God. Readers find *Here and Now* "simple yet profound" and "something that can be read in minutes, and thought about for a lifetime."

For those readers wanting a bit more, Stilwell completed a companion volume called *Living Here and Now: A Practical Guide To Finding Meaning.*

Stilwell's storytelling also produced fifteen plays and two novels. He currently draws meditational cartoons featuring Thrashin' Jack and Lotus the cat. Find them on his Instagram page: JeffStilwellDraws.

Enjoy Jeff Stilwell's meditational drawings further on his Instagram page:
@JeffStilwellDraws.

Jeff is thinking.

Visit Jeff's website: JeffStilwell.com

To invite Jeff onto your show, email him at info@jeffstilwell.com.

Here and Now: A Whimsical Take on God
Book Club Reader's Guide

Chapter One
1. God-making was all the rage in Ur, long long ago. What Gods do you see people creating in our time?

2. What do the Gods people create tell you about those people?

3. What is your favorite comic in Chapter One? Why?

4. Have you ever felt yourself in a similar situation? Tell about that.

Chapter Two
1. What similarities do you notice between the Hebrews, the followers of Jesus and the followers of Mohammed?

2. What differences do you notice between the three groups?

3. What is your favorite comic in Chapter Two? Why?

4. Have you ever felt yourself in a similar situation? Tell about that.

Chapter Three
1. What do you do when you get multiple, competing answers from priests?

2. How do you feel about Heaven being a fantasy? Why?

3. What is your favorite comic in Chapter Three? Why?

4. Have you ever felt yourself in a similar situation? Tell about that.

Chapter Four
1. Are you worried about choosing right from wrong with no God to guide you? Why or why not?

2. How do we explore the fullest expression of meaning in our lives? Name some ways.

3. What is your favorite comic in Chapter Four? Why?

4. Have you ever felt yourself in a similar situation? Tell about that.

Made in United States
Orlando, FL
09 October 2023